W9-BNP-046

FINDING
COMMUNITY

Other Books in the LIVING PROUD! Series

FINDING COMMUNITY

Robert Rodi and Laura Ross

Foreword by Kevin Jennings
Founder, GLSEN (the Gay, Lesbian & Straight
Education Network)

MASON CREST

Mason Crest
450 Parkway Drive, Suite D
Broomall, PA 19008
www.masoncrest.com

Printed in the United States of America

First printing
9 8 7 6 5 4 3 2 1

Series ISBN: 978-1-4222-3501-0
Hardcover ISBN: 978-1-4222-3505-8
ebook ISBN: 978-1-4222-8378-3

Cataloging-in-Publication Data is available on file at the Library of Congress.

Developed and Produced by Print Matters Productions, Inc. (www.printmattersinc.com)
Cover and Interior Design by Kris Tobiassen, Matchbook Digital

Picture credits: 10, franckreporter/iStock; 14, ViewApart/iStock; 15, Peeter Viisimaa/iStock; 16, Frank Buchalski/Wikimedia Creative Commons; 18, Rikke/Shutterstock; 20, U.S. Department of Defense; 25, Terry Schmitt/UPI/Newscom; 27, Joel Carillet/iStock; 28, Chris Freeland/Wikimedia Creative Commons; 30, Wendy Nero/Shutterstock; 32, Rachel Ritchie/KRT/Newscom; 34, Richard B. Levine/Newscom; 37, Eugenio Marongiu/iStock; 38, Lee Snider/Dreamstime; 40, Eldad Carin/iStock; 42, Wikimedia Creative Commons; 45, Frances M. Roberts/Newscom; 48, Shane Keyser/MCT/Newscom; 52, Cat Jerici/Wikimedia Creative Commons
Front cover: Richard B. Levine/Newscom: A mile-long rainbow flag is unfurled in New York City at the Pride Parade marking the 25th anniversary of the Stonewall riots.

FINDING
COMMUNITY

CONTENTS

KEY ICONS TO LOOK FOR

Text-Dependent Questions: These questions send the reader back to the text for more careful attention to the evidence presented there.

Words to Understand: These words with their easy-to-understand definitions will increase the reader's understanding of the text while building vocabulary skills.

Series Glossary of Key Terms: This back-of-the-book glossary contains terminology used throughout this series. Words found here increase the reader's ability to read and comprehend higher-level books and articles in this field.

Research Projects: Readers are pointed toward areas of further inquiry connected to each chapter. Suggestions are provided for projects that encourage deeper research and analysis.

Sidebars: This boxed material within the main text allows readers to build knowledge, gain insights, explore possibilities, and broaden their perspectives by weaving together additional information to provide realistic and holistic perspectives.

FOREWORD

I loved libraries as a kid.

Every Saturday my mom and I would drive from the trailer where we lived on an unpaved road in the unincorporated town of Lewisville, North Carolina, and make the long drive to the "big city" of Winston-Salem to go to the downtown public library, where I would spend joyous hours perusing the books on the shelves. I'd end up lugging home as many books as my arms could carry and generally would devour them over the next seven days, all the while eagerly anticipating next week's trip. The library opened up all kinds of worlds to me—all kinds of worlds, except a gay one.

Oh, I found some "gay" books, even in the dark days of the 1970s. I'm not sure how I did, but I found my way to authors like Tennessee Williams, Yukio Mishima, and Gore Vidal. While these great artists created masterpieces of literature that affirmed that there were indeed other gay people in the universe, their portrayals of often-doomed gay men hardly made me feel hopeful about my future. It was better than nothing, but not much better. I felt so lonely and isolated I attempted to take my own life my junior year of high school.

In the 35 years since I graduated from high school in 1981, much has changed. Gay–straight alliances (an idea my students and I pioneered at Concord Academy in 1988) are now widespread in American schools. Out LGBT (lesbian, gay, bisexual, and transgender) celebrities and programs with LGBT themes are commonplace on the airwaves. Oregon has a proud bisexual governor, multiple members of Congress are out as lesbian, gay, or bisexual, and the White House was bathed in rainbow colors the day marriage equality became the law of the land in 2015. It gets better, indeed.

So why do we need the Living Proud! series?

- Because GLSEN (the Gay, Lesbian & Straight Education Network) reports that over two-thirds of LGBT students routinely hear anti-LGBT language at school.

- Because GLSEN reports that over 60% of LGBT students do not feel safe at school.
- Because the CDC (the Centers for Disease Control and Prevention, a U.S. government agency) reports that lesbian and gay students are four times more likely to attempt suicide than heterosexual students

In my current role as the executive director of the Arcus Foundation (the world's largest financial supporter of LGBT rights), I work in dozens of countries and see how far there still is to go. In over 70 countries same-sex relations are crimes under existing laws: in 8, they are a crime punishable by the death penalty. It's better, but it's not all better—especially in our libraries, where there remains a need for books that address LGBT issues that are appropriate for young people, books that will erase both the sense of isolation so many young LGBT people still feel as well as the ignorance so many non-LGBT young people have, ignorance that leads to the hate and violence that still plagues our community, both at home and abroad.

The Living Proud! series will change that and will save lives. By providing accurate, age-appropriate information to young people of all sexual orientations and gender identities, the Living Proud! series will help young people understand the complexities of the LGBT experience. Young LGBT people will see themselves in its pages, and that reflection will help them see a future full of hope and promise. I wish Living Proud! had been on the shelves of the Winston-Salem/Forsyth County Public Library back in the seventies. It would have changed my life. I'm confident that it will have as big an impact on its readers today as it would have had on me back then. And I commend it to readers of any age.

Kevin Jennings
Founder, GLSEN (the Gay, Lesbian & Straight Education Network)
Executive Director, Arcus Foundation

GLSEN®

GLSEN is the leading national education organization focused on ensuring safe and affirming schools for all students. GLSEN seeks to develop school climates where difference is valued for the positive contribution it makes to creating a more vibrant and diverse community.
www.glsen.org

A community can mean anything from a group of supportive friends to a neighborhood where you feel safe and comfortable being yourself.

1

GAY COMMUNITIES

 WORDS TO UNDERSTAND

Out: For an LGBT person, the state of being open with other people about his or her sexual or gender identity.

Rainbow flag: A symbol of gay pride and welcome.

Minority: A smaller group of people within the larger, majority population who differ from the majority in race, religion, sexual orientation, or other characteristics.

Oppression: Keeping another person or group of people in an inferior position.

LGBT: An acronym or abbreviation for lesbian, gay, bisexual, and transgender. Sometimes a "Q" is added **(LGBTQ)** to stand for "questioning"—which goes to show how much variation there can be in gender identity. "Q" may also stand for "queer."

When Mike was in his first year at the local community college, he announced to his family that he was gay. Fortunately for him, his family was a loving and supportive one (and his father's favorite sister, June, was a proudly **"out"** lesbian). After graduation, he left his little Indiana town and moved into an apartment with a housemate near Wrigley Field in Chicago. Six months later, his younger sister Heather took the bus to the big city to visit Mike for a long weekend. Even though they were seven years apart, they had always been close, and they were both anxious to spend some time together.

"Welcome to Boystown," Mike said with a grin when they got to his neighborhood. It had earned its nickname because of its popularity as a place for gay men to live.

Mike had planned a whole weekend of activities for them: a Cubs game with Mike's roommate (who had more cool piercings and tattoos than Heather had ever seen) and her girlfriend (who had even more); a potluck dinner with the members of Mike's Gay Men's Chorus group; shopping (Mike bought Heather a tee-shirt with the words "Girl Pride" printed in glitter at a little shop on Broadway); and services on Sunday morning at a church where they flew the rainbow flag (a symbol of gay pride), followed by brunch at a restaurant where their waitress was a tall, elegant African-American woman who called everyone "Sweet Thing," and who had been born a man. Heather and Mike had a wonderful time together.

Just before he put Heather on the bus back to Indiana, Mike asked her, "So, what do you think of my community?"

Heather thought for a moment about what his question meant. She thought of the way Mike had left the warm, supportive company of their family and had found an even larger group of welcoming people to live among—his neighborhood, his housemate, his friends, his church, and his favorite restaurant. She thought of how nice everyone had been to her and how happy Mike was in Boystown. She could understand how it might feel like a second family to him.

"I love your community, Mike," she said.

Mike gave Heather a big hug. "So do I, little sister!"

The Human Community

Human beings are social animals. Scientists tell us that our earliest ancestors, like many animal species, lived together in small groups of individuals, many of them related, who cooperated with each other for the common good of the group—protection from danger, cooperation in hunting and food-gathering activities, the sharing of that food, the care of the young. We needed each other to survive in the world, as we still do. Over time, people's concept of what defined their group grew larger, to include their village, their tribe, and eventually their nation. In the 21st century, many people think that the best hope for our future is to expand our understanding of our "group" to include all people on Earth.

As social animals, we live our entire lives among other people; we are happiest when our lives are rich with relationships, when we live in community. The word *community* can mean different things to different people, but basically it refers to a group of individuals who are connected by bonds of respect, along with a shared sense of identity, interests, and values. Often a community is thought to revolve around a specific geographical location—a neighborhood, a town, a city—but that's not always the case.

A community can mean different things, but it is always more than just a random group of people. Those who are part of a particular community are connected to each other in some way—either because they live close together or because they share common interests or identities.

We are born into certain communities that can be very important to our sense of who we are as we grow up: our family, our ethnic or racial heritage, our religious tradition, our hometown, our nation. The traditions and values of these most basic communities shape our view of ourselves and the world.

Throughout American history, ethnic and racial **minority** groups, especially those that have been the victims of prejudice and **oppression,** have formed particularly strong communities. Native Americans, African-Americans, Hispanics, Jews, and new immigrants (at various times comprising the Irish, the Italians, and the Chinese, among others) have stuck

Minority groups often choose to live near each other to give support and identity to their communities. Chinatown in New York City is a good example of this.

together to support one another economically and socially in tough times. These minority groups often chose—and were sometimes forced—to live in close-knit neighborhoods, keeping their traditions and their heritage alive as a matter of pride and group strength.

Ethnic and racial communities still exist in many of America's towns and cities. Likewise, many of our citizens continue to face economic and social disadvantages, and find strength in their community identity.

For some people, the communities they *choose* to become a part of are as important to them as the community into which they were born. These voluntary communities can also be powerful means of support, strength, and happiness for people.

CLOSE-UP: FAMOUS GAY NEIGHBORHOODS

Many urban areas have a district that seems to be predominately LGBT, attracting residents from far and wide. Sometimes affectionately known as "the gay ghetto" or "the gayborhood," these areas have lots of shops, bars, restaurants, and businesses that are either LGBT-friendly or cater directly to an LGBT clientele.

Some of the most famous gay communities can be found in the Castro in San Francisco, Chelsea in New York City, East Lakeview in Chicago (better know as "Boystown"), West Hollywood in Los Angeles, and Montrose in Houston. There are also resort communities that attract largely gay home-owners and visitors, including Provincetown in Massachusetts and Palm Springs in California. Fire Island, just off the coast of Long Island, New York, is notable for two distinctive areas: The Pines, which has for many years been a mecca for gay men, and the adjoining Cherry Grove, which has a similar history for lesbians.

One of the rainbow markers that identifies the Boystown neighborhood in Chicago.

An Invisible Minority

LGBT people are born and grow up in communities just like everybody else, but, unfortunately, some of these communities—families, churches, ethnic groups—have been known to reject and exclude them. While society has been maturing in its attitudes toward **LGBT** people, mostly through the efforts of education and political action by LGBT people themselves, thousands have nevertheless been rejected by their families, their churches, and even their hometowns.

But one of the great strengths of human beings is that even in the midst of oppression and rejection, we continue to seek each other out and build supportive communities, sometimes against great odds.

The Williams Institute at the UCLA School of Law estimates that there are 8.8 million openly gay, lesbian, and bisexual people living in the United States. Various studies have estimated that between one in ten and one in twenty people are "gay," but how the word is defined and how comfortable people are in identifying themselves with that word makes these figures hard to pin down. What is clear is that there are a lot of gay and lesbian people in our country—maybe just as many of them as there are left-handed people! And like left-handed people, gay people are born into all kinds of families in all kinds of places.

Despite what some who subscribe to stereotypes believe, you can't tell if people are gay just by looking at them. They are an invisible minority. But "invisible" or not, gay and lesbian people have always found ways to locate each other and build their own communities.

For LGBT people, "finding each other" is not just about finding a partner; partners also need a larger community to support and understand them.

A young gay person might grow up thinking that he is the only "different" person in the whole world, and this can be scary and depressing. Discovering just one other gay person in his town (or even a gay character in a book or movie) can begin to open up a whole new world and make him feel less alone. If he finds one best friend with whom he can be honest, a few gay friends in his school, a trusted older gay relative, this may be the beginning of his own gay community.

Many people, like Mike in our story, have sought a larger LGBT community in a town or city and have found happiness and self-esteem by associating with large numbers of other LGBT people. The Internet and the growth of social networks, such as Facebook and Twitter, have extended membership in the larger LGBT community to people in rural areas, small towns, and around the world.

LGBT people, like other minority groups, have worked hard to build and strengthen their communities. In the 21st century, there is no longer any reason for LGBT people to feel alone in the world. This community is strong and full of life and energy!

 TEXT-DEPENDENT QUESTIONS

- What makes a community?
- How is the LGBT community different from other minority communities?
- What factors help bring the national LGBT community together in this century?

 RESEARCH PROJECTS

- Make a list of the communities, large and small, that you yourself belong to.
- Find out if you live near a neighborhood that is predominantly one ethnicity, then visit it and look for visible signs of community.
- Visit your nearest LGBT neighborhood, and get a sense of what it feels like to be there.

We Can Do It

World War II opened fresh opportunities to women. The easing of gender restrictions also opened new vistas for the lesbian community.

2

THE FOUNDATIONS OF THE LGBT COMMUNITY

 WORDS TO UNDERSTAND

Nonverbal: Communicated without the use of words.
Gay liberation: The movement for the civil and legal rights of gay people, with origins in the late 1960s and '70s.
Transient: Moving from place to place without strong ties to home.
Conservative: Cautious; resistant to change and new ideas.
Bohemian: Used to describe a neighborhood where the residents are non-traditional in their lifestyle and often interested in the arts and political movements.
Pioneers: People who are the first to try new things and experiment with new ways of life.

Ramona came from a close Mexican-American family in Fresno, California. Growing up in the 1930s, she always felt a little different from her sisters and the other girls in her town, but she tried to fit in and be the young lady her family wanted her to be. At seventeen, she and her brother's best friend, Miguel, got engaged, but she was secretly relieved in 1942 when the war came and Miguel joined the Navy. Although she tried hard to be "normal" and prayed every day to change, Ramona had a very guilty secret: she was sexually and romantically attracted to girls.

With the war on and the men overseas, there were suddenly lots of jobs for women, and Ramona moved to Los Angeles to get a job at an airplane factory where her cousin Maria worked. Ramona loved the freedom of being away from her strict family and the independence of having her own money to spend. She also enjoyed little things like being able to wear jeans and boots and keep her hair short, the way she liked it. She lived in a rooming house with a lot of other girls from all over the country, and, for the first time in her life, she met girls who liked other girls, just as she did.

Ramona and her new friends called themselves "the gay girls" and formed a close group. Some of the other women didn't like them, and called them horrible names. They even pushed them around—but the "gay girls" always stuck up for one another, and Ramona learned she was pretty tough. One night at a bar, Ramona met Helen, a tall, beautiful blond woman from Texas. Within a few weeks, Ramona and Helen were a couple, very much in love. They talked about saving their money and buying a house together after the war—and being together forever. One thing Ramona knew for sure was that she was never going back to Fresno. She'd never marry Miguel. She was a gay girl.

Finding Each Other

Gay men and lesbians have always been able to find one another. The human need for companionship, both social and sexual, is so strong that even against the great odds of oppression and prejudice, people find a way to come together with their own kind. Gay people sometimes talk about "gaydar," the ability to recognize another gay person by a look, a gesture, or just a "sixth sense," and they have relied on that ability to connect in the most oppressive times and places.

Gathering places for gay men have been documented since ancient times. The public baths and gymnasiums of Ancient Rome were well known as places for gay men to meet and socialize. Throughout history, gay men have had the opportunity to meet, often secretly, through traditional all-male organizations such as sports clubs, fraternities, schools, and the military.

As far back as the 1600s, neighborhoods in Amsterdam and London were known for taverns and coffee houses that served as gathering places for homosexual men. These men used a special slang among themselves—a kind of secret code—to keep their identity hidden from the outside world. The word "gay" itself, meaning a homosexual person, may have had its origin in the homosexual slang of the 1700s. Slang, secret symbols, and **nonverbal** communication were all part of navigating the underground gay culture in previous eras.

The early history of the lesbian community is harder to trace. Until relatively recently, women lived in a way that was less public, and more tied to home and family. Their lives were considered less interesting and were consequently less written about than the lives of men.

The advantage that lesbians had over gay men was that they could "hide in plain sight." Two women living together rarely raised eyebrows. It was assumed that they were lonely "spinsters," living together for protection and companionship.

For most gay people in the days before the **gay liberation** movement, their hometowns were difficult and often unhappy places to live. Small-town prejudices, family restrictions, and the judgment of the church kept them from pursuing happy and fulfilling lives for themselves. But some gay people looked for alternatives to the communities into which they were born.

The frontier of the American West in the 1800s, for example, opened up possibilities for gay people, especially men, to escape to a more open and free environment and lifestyle. The tradition of gay cowboys and their "pardners" goes back well before *Brokeback Mountain.* The growing cities of America also offered a certain amount of freedom to gay people. The seaport cities of New Orleans, San Francisco, and New York, with their **transient** populations of single people and open-minded traditions, were especially attractive to gay people (and still are).

In the 1860s, the poet Walt Whitman (who was gay) wrote:

Once I pass'd through a populous city imprinting my brain for future use with its shows, architecture, customs, traditions,
Yet now of all that city I remember only a man I casually met there who detain'd me for love of me.

But of course, few gay people were as freethinking and self-aware as Walt! Most tried to live their lives as best they could in their hometowns, without any kind of gay community to support them.

CLOSE-UP: THE PIONEERING DAUGHTERS OF BILITIS

Taking their name from an 1894 erotic lesbian novel, *The Songs of Bilitis*, the Daughters of Bilitis was one of the first lesbian social and political groups in the world. They met informally in the homes of members and kept their membership list secret, even urging women to attend meetings in traditional feminine clothing so as to avoid harassment by the police. (If you can believe it, in the 1950s it was illegal for women to wear men's clothes in public!)

Membership grew over the years, and the Daughters of Bilitis became a real force in advocating for the acceptance of gay people in society, holding biennial conventions starting in 1960 and publishing a magazine, *The Ladder*, from 1956 to 1972. The group disbanded in the mid-1970s.

On June 16, 2008, Phyllis Lyon (right) and Del Martin (left), the founders of the Daughters of Bilitis, were the first same-sex couple to be married legally in San Francisco. They had been in a committed relationship for fifty-six years and are shown here cutting their wedding cake.

A Changing World

World War II (1939–1945) brought enormous changes to American society—changes that laid the real foundations of what we call the LGBT community. Nearly every young man and many young women between the ages of eighteen and thirty left home to serve in the military, where they were exposed to the company of people from a variety of backgrounds and from all parts of the country. Men from farms and small towns were suddenly exposed to what life was like in the big cities. Women from "respectable, old-fashioned" families made friends with "fast" girls who drank and smoked and never went to church. And with so many men in the Armed Forces, many women left their traditional roles as homemakers to work in war industry factories, affording them economic and social opportunities they had never had before. While the Nazis were exterminating gay people in concentration camps in Europe, millions of gay people in America were discovering their own identities and coming together on a scale never before seen in history.

After the war, most gay and lesbian people went back home to their **conservative** and disapproving communities. But some never did. Gay ex-servicemen and gay women, liberated from traditional roles by war work, settled in the low-rent **bohemian** neighborhoods of the big seaport cities, attracted to the freedom and openness they found there. Neighborhoods such as the French Quarter in New Orleans, Greenwich Village in New York, and the Castro District in San Francisco became magnets for gay people from all over the country in the post-war years.

Neighborhoods, such as the French Quarter in New Orleans, still attract LGBT people from around the country.

It was in the cities of America in the 1950s and '60s that the gay community was born.

Bar Communities

Still lacking legal rights and facing societal prejudices, even the urban **pioneers** of the LGBT community were forced to hide their homosexual identities in all but a few select places. Across America, bars and nightclubs were the only comfortable, indoor meeting places available to most

Bars and dance clubs have always been places where members of the LGBT community found one another.

gay and lesbian people. These bars were often owned by organized-crime figures who took advantage of their gay customers by charging high prices for admission and drinks. Bar owners often paid off the local police in order to offer their customers some protection from legal harassment.

One lesbian woman from New Orleans, now in her eighties, recalls that in the 1950s, "they would flash a light on the dance floor when the police were on the premises, and we would all quickly change dance partners. Being caught dancing with another woman was against the law, and you could be arrested for it."

But despite the payoffs (and warning lights), gay bars were subject to police raids at any time, with gay people being arrested and their names printed in the newspaper. Being arrested in a raid, sometimes just for quietly having a drink with friends, destroyed many peoples' lives and careers.

Many smaller cities didn't even have gay bars; nonetheless gay people developed strategies for meeting up in "regular" establishments. A retired gay professor in Binghamton, New York, remembers the early 1960s: "Thursday night was gay night at the Arlington Hotel Bar. If you wore a red tie, we gay guys would be able to recognize each other."

There were disadvantages, of course, to bars as a meeting place for gay people. The bar culture encouraged heavy alcohol consumption, and the dollars gay customers spent often went into the pockets of criminals. And the bars were never really "safe."

Even more secretive than bars were establishments where men could go to engage in sex with other men right on the premises. Called bathhouses—because the first public baths were built for people without access to indoor plumbing to bathe—they began to spring up in the late nineteenth century. The first recorded raid on a bathhouse was in February 1903, in the basement of the Ariston Hotel in New York City.

CLOSE-UP: SOFTBALL—THE LESBIAN ALTERNATIVE

Older lesbians sometimes joke that they always had an alternative to the bars. As one woman writes, "Joining a woman's softball team was often the first move a new lesbian in town made to meet like-minded women."

Women's softball teams were often a good way for lesbians to meet other lesbians.

Double Lives

The urban gay neighborhoods of the 1950s and '60s may have been places of relative safety and comfort, but police harassment and the very real threat of violence and exposure still haunted the gay people who lived there. Many gays lived what can only be called "double lives," forced to pretend to be straight at their jobs and with their families, only free to express their true selves in the secret world of bars and clubs and on a few streets in their cities.

In many ways, however, these big-city gay people were the lucky ones. In small towns and rural areas, most gay people had few opportunities to meet one another and many lived lonely, unhappy lives hiding their "dirty secret."

Throughout these decades, some gay and lesbian people were thinking about more than just their own happiness. They were beginning to tackle the larger issues of gay civil rights and the acceptance of gay people by society. As early as the 1950s, committed people were forming political groups, such as the Mattachine Society in Los Angeles in 1950 and the Daughters of Bilitis in San Francisco in 1955. Both the urban gay pioneers and early gay political activists were very important in the development of the modern gay community, as would be seen during the gay liberation movement and the AIDS crisis.

CLOSE-UP: UNMASKING THE MATTACHINE SOCIETY

One of the country's earliest gay-rights organizations—preceded only by the much shorter-lived Society for Human Rights in the '20s— the Mattachine Society was founded in 1950 and derived its name from a brotherhood of masked players in medieval France, the Société Mattachine. (This was a reference to the public "mask" of homosexuality.)

Its founder, Harry Hay, was quite publicly gay, and modeled the Los Angeles–based group's operations on the American Communist Party, of which he was a member. But the extreme anti-Communism of the succeeding decade caused the group to restructure along more traditional lines, and Hay himself stepped down as the Society's leader.

Mattachine Society founder Harry Hay, shown here at age 84, said, "My brothers and sisters, I want them all to grow to their full capacity. But I want them to grow to their full gay capacity."

The group soon boasted chapters in a number of American cities, but divisions among them caused the national organization to splinter. In the 1960s, newer, bolder, and more progressive gay-rights groups dismissed the Mattachine's brand of activism as too cautious and conservative; however, the organization's courage in campaigning for gay equality in what was arguably the country's most viciously conformist decade, demands respect and gratitude.

 TEXT-DEPENDENT QUESTIONS

- How did the new frontier of the American West help gay people discover one another?

- How did America's urban centers help gay people discover one another in the 19th and early 20th centuries?

- How has our military helped gay people discover one another?

 RESEARCH PROJECTS

- Read some memoirs of gay and lesbian life in the 1920s through the 1960s.

- Explore more deeply, online, the campaigns and activities of the Mattachine Society and Daughters of Bilitis.

- If you know any LGBT people who were around in the early decades of the last century, ask them about their recollections and experiences.

A Gay Men's Health Crisis poster in a New York City subway station is aimed at black and Latino men, encouraging pride in gay men of color and promoting HIV testing.

3

GAY LIBERATION AND AIDS

 WORDS TO UNDERSTAND

Mainstream: Something that is accepted, understood, and supported by the majority of people.

Civil rights: The rights of a citizen to personal and political freedom under the law.

Politicized: Aware of one's rights and willing to demand them through political action.

Collective: A group where the needs and desires of the entire membership are considered.

Cooperative: People working together rather than in competition.

Radical: Someone who has extreme, out-of-the-ordinary ideas and beliefs.

Stigma: A mark of shame.

Epidemic: A widespread outbreak of a disease.

Frank left Georgia on his twenty-second birthday, May 14, 1977, and never looked back. He had left a good job at his father's insurance agency, and his mother had told him he was breaking her heart—but he loved living in San Francisco. Even though he was not making much money working as a waiter ("wasting his education at the best Christian College in the South," his father said) and was living in a tiny apartment in a run-down neighborhood, Frank felt like the luckiest guy in the world as he dressed for his friend Steve's party.

He put a Village People record on the turntable and danced to "Macho Man" as he got ready, blow-drying his hair, trimming his mustache, and laying out his Levis, his tightest tee shirt, and his brand-new black leather bomber jacket. He was a little nervous because he knew there would be at least two of his old boyfriends at Steve's—but hey, he sure wasn't going to miss one of the hottest parties of the year. And tomorrow was the Gay Pride Parade in the Castro District! Oh, if they could only see him now back in Decatur! It was great to be gay!

Stonewall and the LGBT Civil Rights Movement

The last forty years have seen an incredible transformation in LGBT communities, moving them out of the shadows and into the mainstream of American life. The struggle for LGBT rights and the huge challenges of the AIDS crisis were two of the major forces at work in defining gay identity, strengthening communities, and building understanding between straight and gay people.

In 1969, it was illegal for people of the same sex to dance together in a public place, hold hands, or wear clothes that were not considered "normal" for their sex. Undercover police would go into bars and clubs, observe these behaviors, and close the place down. The liquor

CLOSE-UP: ONLINE LGBT COMMUNITIES

The digital revolution hasn't just transformed the way gay people hook up with each other; it's also transformed the whole idea of an LGBT community, allowing for connections that were either difficult or impossible to make before. Not only have the major gay periodicals established an on-line presence—including influential magazines such as *The Advocate* and the *Washington Blade*, the country's oldest LGBT newspaper—but original web pages offer a wide range of insights and opinions, as well as oppor-tunities for chat and networking. Sites such as GaySpeak, Empty Closets, and Gay Bros cater to different sensibilities and needs, and there are many others to explore, running the gamut of the LGBT experience.

Online communities and dating sites and apps have dramatically expanded the ability of LGBT people to meet one another.

The Stonewall Inn in New York City remains a symbol of the struggle for LGBT rights.

was confiscated, and if they weren't lucky enough to slip out the back door, LGBT people were subject to arrest for "disorderly conduct" or "lewd behavior," with their names listed in the newspaper. The average New York gay bar was raided once a month during the 1960s, and the authorities were constantly bullying gay people.

At 1:20 a.m. on June 28, 1969, the police raided the Stonewall Inn in Greenwich Village, New York City. But this night was different. Gathering on the street in front of the Stonewall, a group of angry people—including a number of transgender people and "drag queens" who had been particularly frequent victims of the police—refused to be bullied. Fights broke out between the police and the crowd, windows were broken, parking meters smashed, and many arrests were made in what became known as the "Stonewall Riots." The story made front-page news across the country. For several nights in a row, groups of young LGBT people marched through the streets of Greenwich Village expressing their anger and frustration.

Many historians consider the Stonewall Riots the beginning of the modern gay rights movement. Within days of the riots, a new political action group was formed in New York. Unlike the more coded names adopted by earlier homosexual rights groups, such as the Mattachine Society and Daughters of Bilitis, this one was proudly called the Gay Liberation Front.

Gay Pride marches were organized in New York, Chicago, and Los Angeles on June 28, 1970, the one-year anniversary of Stonewall. The following year, similar events took place in Boston, Dallas, Milwaukee, San Francisco, London, Paris, Berlin, and Stockholm. These marches were a call for the recognition of the gay community, a show of gay pride, and a demand for civil rights.

Many LGBT people became **politicized** in the 1970s, starting gay rights organizations and support groups in towns and cities and on college campuses, expressing themselves in newly formed gay newspapers and magazines, and in public marches and rallies. Gay people were coming out in huge numbers and urging other gay people to do the same.

CLOSE-UP: GAY PRIDE IS GLOBAL

Today, there are literally thousands of Gay Pride parades and festivals across the world; for example, more than half a million people participate in the Gay and Lesbian Mardi Gras in Sydney, Australia, the largest gay pride event in the world. June is officially Gay Pride month in many places, honoring the movement that was born when that first group of LGBT people stood up to the police at the Stonewall Inn in 1969.

People celebrating at the annual gay pride parade in Tel Aviv, Israel.

An Ongoing Party

After so many years of oppression and secrecy, it was a time of great excitement, freedom, and pride for LGBT people. Young gay people flocked to the cities, bringing new energy to the older gay neighborhoods and establishing new ones. Bars and clubs (no longer controlled by organized crime but with proud gay owners) and gay-owned businesses thrived. To the beat of disco music, LGBT people danced (together!) in a celebration of fun and freedom.

"It was one big party," says one gay man remembering the 1970s, "the biggest party you could imagine."

The capital of Gay America in the 1970s was the Castro Street neighborhood in San Francisco, "a city known for its freedom" according to a song by the Village People, a popular music group of the time. Packed into a few square blocks were thousands of young gay men, the so-called "Castro Clones" (the East Coast versions were the "Christopher Street Clones" of New York) in their uniform of Levi's jeans, tight shirts, and black leather jackets. They rejected the old "sissy" stereotypes of the past and boldly proclaimed their new image to the world.

With a growing presence and increasing voting power, gays in San Francisco began flexing their political muscle. It was in San Francisco in 1977 that Harvey Milk, the subject of the 2009 film *Milk*, was elected to the position of City Supervisor, the first openly gay person elected to public office in the United States. (Tragically, he was assassinated eleven months later by a deeply disturbed and prejudiced coworker in city government.)

Harvey Milk was the first openly gay person elected to a public office in the United States.

In other American cities, gay people created their own local versions of the Castro, often moving into run-down inner-city areas, buying and fixing up inexpensive houses, and generally cleaning up the neighborhood in a process called "gentrification." At a time when many American cities were in serious decline, gay people brought a new energy and commitment to urban living that helped reverse a downward trend.

On college campuses across the country, gay and lesbian students came together for discussions (called "rap groups"), political action, and social activities. At many colleges, the gay organization's dances were the most popular on campus, bringing gay and straight people together in a spirit of fun. Meanwhile, the media was catching on to the new visibility of the gay community, and gay and lesbian characters were regularly portrayed in movies and on television—not without stereotypes, but at least right there in the open. In small towns and rural areas, media coverage of gay life was giving LGBT people a sense that there was a world out there for them, too.

Lesbians in the 1970s

Sometimes frustrated by the continued dominance of men in the gay liberation movement, many gay women created their own communities in the seventies. Women communicated through their own publications with in-your-face names, such as *Lesbians Fight Back*, *Sinister Women*, and *Salsa Soul Sisters/Third World Women's Gay-zette*. Lesbians formed their own support groups and community centers and hung out together in their own bars and restaurants. Politics among gay women tended to be more **collective** and **cooperative**, as they fought a double oppression as both women and lesbians. Bringing a particularly **radical** approach to the growing women's liberation movement, some lesbians worked toward building a society completely separate from men and completely free of men's power and control.

The End of the Party

The 1970s were a time of incredible experimentation in lifestyle, politics, and identity formation for gay people. Out of the closet for the first time in large numbers, gays reinvented themselves free of society's stereotypes, creating their own new communities. And then disaster struck.

"AIDS ended the party," as the saying goes in the gay community. In the summer of 1981, an article appeared in the *New York Times* about a mysterious new disease that was affecting gay men in New York and San Francisco. The symptoms were horrifying: skin cancers, infection, intense pain, pneumonia, and death. Within months, dozens of gay men were sick and dying, and the gay community was terrified. At first called "gay cancer" and later GRID (Gay-Related Immune Deficiency), it quickly became identified as a "gay" disease.

Because there was no known cause or treatment, the medical care for early victims of the disease was disgraceful. People lay in agony in hospital beds, covered in their own feces, while hospital staff, including nurses and doctors, refused to enter their rooms for fear of catching AIDS. As the 1980s progressed, more and more gay men became sick, and the death toll climbed. There were 16,000 reported AIDS cases by 1985.

"It seemed like overnight everyone I knew was getting sick," remembers a San Francisco man. "You'd run into guys on the street who six months before were the hottest men in the Castro . . . walking with canes and looking like skeletons. All I could think of was, was I next?"

Carrying the powerful **stigma** of having a "gay" disease, AIDS sufferers were the victims of tremendous prejudice. Sick people were evicted from their apartments, fired from their jobs, disowned by their families, and

CLOSE-UP: ACT UP TAKES ACTION

Frustrated and angered by the lack of government action in educating the general public about HIV/AIDS and in funding research and social programs, the AIDS Coalition to Unleash Power (ACT UP) was organized in 1987. The members of ACT UP were gay and proud and radical in their activities; they demanded to be heard, demanded that people with HIV/AIDS and their needs be taken seriously, and demanded that LGBT people have the same rights as any other citizen of the United States. They were committed to political action directed toward politicians and government agencies and to high-impact educational programs. More than a quarter-century later, they are still at it!

Hundreds of members of ACT UP (AIDS Coalition to Unleash Power) protest the lack of an effective treatment for AIDS by holding a "die-in" on Fifth Avenue in New York City in 1990.

refused treatment by medical personnel. Because the general public believed the disease affected mostly gay men and drug addicts, it was slow to show any concern for people with AIDS, and the government dragged its feet for years in funding AIDS medical research and programs to help sick people. It seemed as if gay men with AIDS were being abandoned by society.

But their community did not abandon them.

 CLOSE-UP: AIDS AND THE END OF BATHHOUSES

In the free-wheeling sixties, bathhouses were celebrated as temples of the unhindered libido, but the AIDS crisis dealt them a killing blow. By allowing for multiple anonymous partners, they helped to spread the HIV virus. A few bathhouses still linger in major cities, but gay men seeking new and immediate sex partners are many times more likely to use hookup apps on their smart phones. Similarly, easy access to online pornography caused the withering away of gay adult bookstores and theaters, which had sprung up in the more permissive legal atmosphere of the sixties, and which had also functioned as arenas for sexual contact.

Early in the AIDS **epidemic**, informal groups of friends—and, later, organized volunteers called "AIDS buddies"—helped to care for the sick men of the gay community. Cleaning apartments, walking dogs, grocery shopping, and preparing meals, these buddies brought friendship and compassionate care to people who needed it. Despite their own health fears, AIDS buddies bravely faced the challenges of caring for their own people.

While government agencies and society in general stood by, gay people donated their own time, talent, and money in the fight against AIDS and the care of those affected by AIDS. The Gay Men's Health Crisis (GMHC) was founded by a group of gay doctors and community leaders in New York City in January of 1982. It was the world's first—and would become the leading provider—of HIV/AIDS education, prevention, and care.

With advances in medical science and HIV/AIDS prevention education, AIDS is no longer the fatal disease it once was in the gay men's community. Today, it is a treatable condition—and a preventable one. But while it was raging in the gay community, it killed over 100,000 gay people, and the community has tragically lost a significant percentage of men who would now be in their forties, fifties, and sixties. Nevertheless, the modern gay community that was born at the height of the gay liberation movement, only to be challenged by the AIDS epidemic, entered the 21st century strong and proud and growing.

 TEXT-DEPENDENT QUESTIONS

- Why is Stonewall called the beginning of the gay liberation movement?
- How did the AIDS epidemic negatively affect the gay rights movement?
- How did awareness of the AIDS epidemic ultimately benefit the gay rights movement?

 RESEARCH PROJECTS

- Find and read some first-hand accounts of the Stonewall Riots.
- Read some of the many AIDS memoirs that are available, with an eye toward learning how the epidemic both devastated and galvanized the community.
- Again, if you know any older LGBT people, interview them about their experiences and memories of this period.

Defensive lineman Michael Sam was the first openly gay football player to be drafted into the NFL

4

GOING MAINSTREAM

 WORDS TO UNDERSTAND

Visibility: The ability to be seen by everyone.
Polls: Scientifically gathered data charting people's opinions.
Diverse: In the case of a community, one that is made up of people from many different backgrounds.
Subculture: A group of people with similar interests and lifestyle within a larger group.

Cheri and Fran had been together for more than twenty years when marriage equality was achieved in Massachusetts. At Thanksgiving dinner in 2009, with their children Will and Eva and many friends and family present, they announced that they would be getting married that spring.

Sixteen-year-old Will is the biological son of Fran and Tom, Cheri and Fran's best friend—nicknamed "Griz" because he is a big, gay Bear—while eleven-year-old Eva was adopted as a baby from China. Fran kept a blog for six months all about the wedding preparations, and Cheri was in constant contact with her Facebook friends the whole time.

The wedding took place on a beautiful May morning at Cheri and Fran's cottage in the Berkshire Mountains. Cheri's Aunt Betty, a Unitarian minister, performed the ceremony, which was attended by most of the members of Fran's Berkshire Women's Hiking Club, the Gay and Lesbian Families Organization of Western Massachusetts, the PTA of Eva's middle school, the Greenefield Gourmet Society, and many family members and friends. During the wedding reception at the local Episcopal Church hall, Will texted his friend Julie in Boston, whose two dads had gotten married a few months before: "u are right! they do look like the 2 happiest women in America. but they wouldn't let me drink any champagne."

LGBT People Are Everywhere!

The LGBT community has gone mainstream in the 21st century. Although still facing major challenges from conservative religious and political groups, the LGBT community has been growing in numbers, political power, and **visibility** as more and more people come out and claim their place in society. No longer a "hidden" minority, out LGBT people are everywhere—on TV, in movies, in almost everybody's family, in every town, in every school: *everywhere.*

And outside the big cities where LGBT communities first organized, LGBT people are living proud, happy, and fulfilling lives in rural areas and small towns across America. Building on the foundations of pioneers of the past, LGBT people today are enjoying a freedom and a sense of pride they have never had before, despite a continuing battle for civil rights and social acceptance that sometimes seems like it will never end.

Gallup **polls** clearly show that the majority of young people find LGBT lifestyles completely acceptable. A significant percentage of people under thirty fully approve of marriage equality and LGBT people serving openly in the military. Times are changing, and are likely to continue to change as the older generation and the prejudices of the past lose their influence.

Getting to Know Each Other

Living proudly and openly, LGBT people can serve as role models for one another—and for the straight people in their lives, too. History has shown us that when people get acquainted on a personal level, as friends, coworkers, and classmates, walls of misunderstanding and prejudice begin to crumble, and stereotypes lose their power. Real progress can be made in building strong, **diverse** communities when people learn to respect and understand one another despite their differences. This is one of the most important lessons of all civil rights movements.

In cities and towns everywhere, LGBT people are active and valued members of their community. Since Harvey Milk's election to city supervisor in San Francisco in 1977, hundreds of openly gay and lesbian people have been elected to office at all levels of government, including Barney Frank, a U.S. Congressman from Massachusetts; Tammy Baldwin, a U.S. Senator from Wisconsin; and Annise Parker, the Mayor of Houston, Texas. Out LGBT people contribute their talents and energy to their hometowns in all kinds of ways, serving on school boards and church councils, as Little League coaches, and as volunteers in homeless shelters. In modern America, LGBT and straight people live and work side by side, send their children to school together, socialize together, and belong to the same clubs, sports teams, and community organizations. LGBT people have become a part of just about everybody's everyday lives.

The Battle's Not Over

Nonetheless, LGBT people are still a minority group, and they are still fighting the battle for full social acceptance and civil rights that they have been fighting for decades. Political organizations and civil rights groups at the national, state, and local level are still very important to the LGBT movement. The Human Rights Campaign, headquartered in Washington, D.C., has over 750,000 members and supporters, and the organizing and fund raising efforts of LGBT people in support of Barack Obama played

"Gay Day" at Walt Disney World.

no small part in electing the first African-American President in history. LGBT people vote for politicians who are responding to their concerns and issues, and politicians are learning to take those votes seriously. More and more Americans are coming to understand that LGBT people deserve all of the same legal rights that straight citizens enjoy.

Still Having Fun

Going mainstream doesn't mean that LGBT people don't still enjoy spending time together and the opportunity to be themselves in their own spaces! A quick glance at the listings in any LGBT community newspaper, such as the *Vital VOICE* from Saint Louis, shows a community that likes to get together and have fun. There are clubs for gay men who play rugby and lesbians who ride mountain bikes, for LGBT Catholics and Latino/Latina Youth, for gay families with children, men who like to wrestle, and women who like to read Jane Austen novels. Bars, coffee houses, and restaurants catering to the community do a thriving business, while LGBT people play and party together on LGBT-friendly cruises and resorts in such places as Key West, Florida, and the Russian River in California.

As more and more people have come out, the LGBT community itself has been learning just how diverse it really is. Many bigger, "furrier," traditionally masculine gay men have had a second coming out as Bears, a lively **subculture** within the community, with its own hangouts and recreational activities. The Rainbow Alliance of the Deaf has chapters all across the country. Gay teenagers and their friends meet through Gay-Straight Alliance clubs that have been organized in hundreds of high schools. And older LGBT people gather together at places like the Golden Rainbow

Senior Center in Palm Springs, California. The gay community is a richly diverse one!

 CLOSE-UP: LGBT SPORTS ORGANIZATIONS

An increasingly popular way for LGBT people to socialize, post-AIDS, is through competitive sports leagues. And while such organizations can be found in nearly every major city and state, there are also now regional, national, and even international groups set up to help operate and promote them.

The Chicago Metropolitan Sports Association is the largest not-for-profit gay and lesbian sports organization in the Midwest. The San Francisco Track and Field Club is a West Coast analogue, and New York is home to several sport-specific groups, such as the Big Apple Softball League, the New York Basketball Association, and Team New York Aquatics. The Gay and Lesbian Athletics Foundation operates at the national level, and the International Gay Rugby Association on a global one. All offer LGBT people—who are often excluded from traditional school sports—a chance to participate in team athletics. And of course, every four years, the Gay Games gives individual LGBT athletes a chance to literally go for the Gold.

An Increasingly Digital Community

The Internet, with its social networking sites and LGBT "cyber communities," is adding new life to the community as well. LGBT people were pioneers in communicating with each other electronically. The Bear community, for example, organized and grew in the 1990s through the online Bear Mailing List. LGBT people in small towns and rural areas discovered one another and their links to the larger gay community by visiting websites and making friends in chat rooms and by e-mail. And while young people have to be especially careful to protect their safety and identity online, some LGBT youth get needed support and encouragement from their online and texting friends—support and encouragement they may not be getting from their families or at school. Like straight people, LGBT adults enjoy meeting through dating sites and personal ads.

Thanks to the hard work, pride, and sacrifices of LGBT people and communities of the past and present, young people today are growing up in a world where they can live full and happy lives in a way that earlier generations could only dream of. While LGBT people still face prejudice and misunderstanding, there are many, many reasons why a young LGBT person should never have to feel alone, "abnormal," or hopeless. Millions before them have helped to build strong and supportive communities and fight for their rights. A rich and diverse LGBT community is out there waiting to welcome a new generation, to teach them, and to learn from them.

 TEXT-DEPENDENT QUESTIONS

- What factors make people today more accepting of LGBT people than they were twenty-five years ago?
- What institutions have sprung up to serve and inform the LGBT community?
- What does "diversity" mean within the LGBT community?

 RESEARCH PROJECTS

- If you have a chance, attend a gay wedding, an LGBT-league softball game or bowling night, or some other similar event.
- List some of the smaller sub-communities within the broader, national LGBT community.
- List some of the ways the tech revolution of the past twenty years has changed the concept of an LGBT community.

🔳 SERIES GLOSSARY

Activists: People committed to social change through political and personal action.

Advocacy: The process of supporting the rights of a group of people and speaking out on their behalf.

Alienation: A feeling of separation and distance from other people and from society.

Allies: People who support others in a cause.

Ambiguous: Something unclear or confusing.

Anonymous: Being unknown; having no one know who you are.

Assumption: A conclusion drawn without the benefit of real evidence.

Backlash: An adverse reaction by a large number of people, especially to a social or political development.

Bias: A tendency or preference toward a particular perspective or ideology that interferes with the ability to be impartial, unprejudiced, or objective.

Bigotry: Stubborn and complete intolerance of a religion, appearance, belief, or ethnic background that differs from one's own.

Binary: A system made up of two, and only two, parts.

Bohemian: Used to describe movements, people, or places characterized by nontraditional values and ways of life often coupled with an interest in the arts and political movements.

Caricature: An exaggerated representation of a person.

Celibate: Choosing not to have sex.

Chromosome: A microscopic thread of genes within a cell that carries all the information determining what a person is like, including his or her sex.

Cisgender: Someone who self-identifies with the gender he or she was assigned at birth.

Civil rights: The rights of a citizen to personal and political freedom under the law.

Clichés: Expressions that have become so overused—stereotypes, for example—that they tend to be used without thought.

Closeted: Choosing to conceal one's true sexual orientation or gender identity.

Compensating: Making up for something by trying harder or going further in the opposite direction.

Conservative: Cautious; resistant to change and new ideas.

Controversy: A disagreement, often involving a touchy subject about which differing opinions create tension and strong reactions.

Customs: Ideas and ways of doing things that are commonly understood and shared within a society.

Demonize: Portray something or someone as evil.

Denominations: Large groups of religious congregations united under a common faith and name, and organized under a single legal administration.

Derogatory: Critical or cruel, as in a term used to make a person feel devalued or humiliated.

Deviation: Something abnormal; something that has moved away from the standard.

Dichotomy: Division into two opposite and contradictory groups.

Discrimination: When someone is treated differently because of his or her race, sexual orientation, gender identity, religion, or some other factor.

Disproportionate: A situation where one particular group is overrepresented within a larger group.

Diverse: In the case of a community, one that is made up of people from many different backgrounds.

Effeminate: A word used to refer to men who have so-called feminine qualities.

Emasculated: Having had one's masculinity or manhood taken away.

Empathy: Feeling for another person; putting yourself mentally and emotionally in another person's place.

Empirical evidence: Factual data gathered from direct observation.

Empowering: Providing strength and energy; making someone feel powerful.

Endocrinologist: A medical doctor who specializes in the treatment of hormonal issues.

Epithets: Words or terms used in a derogatory way to put a person down.

The Establishment: The people who hold influence and power in society.

Extremist: Someone who is in favor of using extreme or radical measures, especially in politics and religion.

Flamboyant: Colorful and a bit outrageous.

Fundamentalist: Someone who believes in a particular religion's fundamental principles and follows them rigidly. When the word is used in connection with Christianity, it refers to a member of a form of Protestant Christianity that believes in the strict and literal interpretation of the Bible.

Gay liberation: The movement for the civil and legal rights of gay people that originated in the 1950s and emerged as a potent force for social and political change in the late 1960s and '70s.

Gender: A constructed sexual identity, whether masculine, feminine, or entirely different.

Gender identity: A person's self-image as female, male, or something entirely different, no matter what gender a person was assigned at birth.

Gender roles: Those activities and traits that are considered appropriate to males and females within a given culture.

Gene: A microscopic sequence of DNA located within a chromosome that determines a particular biological characteristic, such as eye color.

Genitalia: The scientific term for the male and female sex organs.

Genocide: The large-scale murder and destruction of a particular group of people.

Grassroots: At a local level; usually used in reference to political action that begins within a community rather than on a national or global scale.

Harassed/harassment: Being teased, bullied, or physically threatened.

Hate crime: An illegal act in which the victim is targeted because of his or her race, religion, sexual orientation, or gender identity.

Homoerotic: Having to do with homosexual, or same-sex, love and desire.

Homophobia: The fear and hatred of homosexuality. A homophobic person is sometimes referred to as a "homophobe."

Horizontal hostility: Negative feeling among people within the same minority group.

Hormones: Chemicals produced by the body that regulate biological functions, including male and female gender traits, such as beard growth and breast development.

Identity: The way a person, or a group of people, defines and understands who they are.

Inborn: Traits, whether visible or not, that are a part of who we are at birth.

Inclusive: Open to all ideas and points of view.

Inhibitions: Feelings of guilt and shame that keep us from doing things we might otherwise want to do.

Internalized: Taken in; for example, when a person believes the negative opinions other people have of him, he has *internalized* their point of view and made it his own.

Interpretation: A particular way of understanding something.

Intervention: An organized effort to help people by changing their attitudes or behavior.

Karma: The force, recognized by both Hindus and Buddhists, that emanates from one's actions in this life; the concept that the good and bad things one does determine where he or she will end up in the next life.

Legitimized: Being taken seriously and having the support of large numbers of people.

LGBT: An initialism that stands for lesbian, gay, bisexual, and transgender. Sometimes a "Q" is added (**LGBTQ**) to include "questioning." "Q" may also stand for "queer."

Liberal: Open to new ideas; progressive; accepting and supportive of the ideas or identity of others.

Liberation: The act of being set free from oppression and persecution.

Mainstream: Accepted, understood, and supported by the majority of people.

Malpractice: When a doctor or other professional gives bad advice or treatment, either out of ignorance or deliberately.

Marginalize: Push someone to the sidelines, away from the rest of the world.

Mentor: Someone who teaches and offers support to another, often younger, person.

Monogamous: Having only one sexual or romantic partner.

Oppress: Keep another person or group of people in an inferior position.

Ostracized: Excluded from the rest of a group.

Out: For an LGBT person, the state of being open with other people about his or her sexual orientation or gender identity.

Outed: Revealed or exposed as LGBT against one's will.

Persona: A character or personality chosen by a person to change the way others perceive them.

Pioneers: People who are the first to try new things and experiment with new ways of life.

Politicized: Aware of one's rights and willing to demand them through political action.

Prejudice: An opinion (usually unfavorable) of a person or a group of people not based on actual knowledge.

Proactive: Taking action taken in advance of an anticipated situation or difficulty.

Progressive: Supporting human freedom and progress.

Psychologists and psychiatrists: Professionals who study the human mind and human behavior. Psychiatrists are medical doctors who can prescribe pills, whereas clinical psychologists provide talk therapy.

Quackery: When an untrained person gives medical advice or treatment, pretending to be a doctor or other medical expert.

The Right: In politics and religion, the side that is generally against social change and new ideas; often used interchangeably with *conservative.*

Segregation: Historically, a system of laws and customs that limited African Americans' access to many businesses, public spaces, schools, and neighborhoods that were "white only."

Sexual orientation: A person's physical and emotional attraction to the opposite sex (heterosexuality), the same sex (homosexuality), both sexes (bisexuality), or neither (asexuality).

Sociologists: People who study the way groups of humans behave.

Spectrum: A wide range of variations.

Stereotype: A caricature; a way to judge someone, probably unfairly, based on opinions you may have about a particular group they belong to.

Stigma: A mark of shame.

Subculture: A smaller group of people with similar interests and lifestyles within a larger group.

Taboo: Something that is forbidden.

Theories: Ideas or explanations based on research, experimentation, and evidence.

Tolerance: Acceptance of, and respect for, other people's differences.

Transgender: People who identify with a gender different from the one they were assigned at birth.

Transphobia: Fear or hatred of transgender people.

Variance: A range of differences within a category such as gender.

Victimized: Subjected to unfair and negative treatment, including violence, bullying, harassment, or prejudice.

FURTHER RESOURCES

Gay Community and Its Straight Neighbors
Some rules for straights living in a "gayborhood."
gawker.com/5511796/a-contract-between-the-gay-community-and-our-straight-neighbors

The Castro District
A profile of the gayest neighborhood in America.
http://www.sfgate.com/neighborhoods/sf/castro/

Lesbians in World War II
A look back at how the war helped queer women find themselves.
http://www.outhistory.org/exhibits/show/lesbians-20th-century/wwii-beyond

ACT UP
The home page of the pioneering AIDS activist organization.
http://www.actupny.org

The Advocate
The long-running and influential gay news and entertainment magazine.
http://www.advocate.com

The Washington Blade
The nation's oldest LGBT newspaper, and still one of the widest reaching.
http://www.washingtonblade.com

GaySpeak
Friendly forums for gay, bi, curious, or gay-friendly men, women, and teens.
gayspeak.com

Empty Closets
Coming-out resources and chat rooms for LGBT people of all ages.
emptyclosets.com

Gay Bros
A sub-Reddit for gay men who gravitate toward traditionally masculine interests.
http://www.reddit.com/r/gaybros/

Gay-Straight Alliance Resources
Empowering youth activists to fight homophobia and transphobia in schools.
gsanetwork.org/resources

The Human Rights Campaign
The country's premier organization working for LGBT equal rights.
http://www.hrc.org

Gay and Lesbian Athletics Foundation
Dedicated to the acceptance of LGBT people in athletic communities.
glaf.org

INDEX